From Windmills to the World Trade Center:

A Walking Guide to Lower Manhattan History

by Joyce Gold

The cover is a detail from the Duke's Plan, a map drawn for James, Duke of York and Albany, about 1664, depicting New Amsterdam September 16, 1661.

ACKNOWLEDGMENTS

I am very grateful to Alma Routsong, Steve Laise, Val Ginter, and, most especially, Linda Elsroad, for help and support in producing this book.

Old Warren Road Press

Second Edition 1988

All inquiries should be addressed to Old Warren Road Press, 141 W. 17th St., 5th Floor, New York, New York 10011.

ISBN 0-961-0858-1-9

Introduction

Fig. 1. City of New Amsterdam, 1653

The Dutch colony of New Amsterdam on the southern tip of Manhattan Island was a modest imitation of Holland come to the wilderness. The highest point in town in 1664 was a two-story windmill. It was used to grind grain into flour, its loft occasionally serving as a meeting house. Houses were one, two, or three stories and were made of wood, or, more usually, of red, black, or yellow brick brought from Holland as ship's ballast. Behind the houses the settlers kept gardens, where they grew vegetables and fruit trees. In 1664 the population of this Dutch colony was 1500.

The majority of these settlers were not Dutch: Holland was much too prosperous at that time for many natives to emigrate, so mostly alien immigrants to Holland--refugee Protestants, Walloons, and French--settled in Manhattan. In 1643, the 800 Manhattan inhabitants spoke eighteen languages.

Fig. 2. Indians of 1626 from the first known picture of what is now New York

On most of the island, Indians hunted deer, fox and bear in forests seventy to eighty feet high, and caught trout, perch, or beaver in dozens of ponds and streams. A wall separated this wilderness from the town. Made of logs eighteen inches wide and twelve to thirteen feet high with points shaved at the top, the wall crossed the island from river to river and contained two gates--the land gate at today's Broadway, and the water gate at Pearl Street. When Cromwell in England declared war on the Dutch Republic in 1653, the wall was erected to protect New Amsterdam from its nearest warlike British neighbor, at New Haven, Connecticut.

Fig. 3. The Wall

As they had dug canals in Holland, so the colonists excavated a canal up the middle of New Amsterdam. As the Dutch had created land from the sea in Holland, so the colonists began tossing dirt dug for house foundations into the rivers to begin an extensive process of filling in land that continues even today with Battery Park City.

Many of today's Lower Manhattan

streets were laid out and named by these early Dutch. Today's street names are mainly translations into English of the original Dutch names. What had been part of the market is today Marketfeld Street. The place where beaver were caught at the confluence of two canals is now Beaver Street. The street that replaced the wall in 1699 to make room for the growth of the city is now Wall Street.

Chronology

Several European explorers visted Manhattan before the first settlement. The first, in 1524 under the French flag of Francis I, was the Italian Giovanni da Verrazano. After having sailed into New York Bay as far as the Narrows, that place where Staten Island and Long Island come closest to each other, he soon turned around and left because a storm arose. In 1609 the English Henry Hudson, who had been hired by the profit-making Dutch East India Co. to find a route to the Orient, came further inland--as far as the

river now named for him; but he

Fig. 4. Hudson's ship Half Moon

returned to sea upon finding that the river did not lead to the East. He reported favorably on living conditions, farming, trapping, and trading with the Indians.

Once settlers came to the island, the character of Lower Manhattan changed repeatedly. The first eight European settlers arrived in 1624 and settled in the southern tip of the island the Indians called "Man-a-hatta," or "Island of Hills." The colony was ruled by the Dutch West India Co. until 1664, when by merely threatening New Amsterdam with ship guns, the British

Fig. 5. New York City, 1789

took over the island. With a brief interruption in 1674-76, they remained in charge for 119 years, until the end of the American Revolution in 1783. Over the next century and a half, largely because of heavy immigration from around the world, the population of Manhattan grew. The people moved their homes north up the island until only the financial community remained where the first settlement had been.

The tour presented in this book describes how the early settlers and later inhabitants built the tip of Manhattan into what we know today.

1. Trinity Church, Wall St. and Broadway

At what would have been the northern border of New Amsterdam is Trinity Church, the third to occupy this site. The first church of the city's oldest Episcopal parish was built in 1698 on the site of the wall that was removed to allow for the growth of the city. Many local citizens contributed to the first building fund for the official church of the British: Jewish residents supported the official church, which was required by law; Captain William Kidd of Hanover Square lent his block and tackle to the construction a few years before being hanged as a pirate. The first Trinity Church was small and squared-shaped. It faced not Broadway but the more important direction in that mercantile age, the Hudson

Fig. 6. Trinity Church, the first building

River. Trinity received a large land grant from Queen Anne in 1705. It spanned from Rector Street north to Christopher Street; its value has helped support the parish since those early times. The first church was destroyed in 1776, when it went up in flames in a great fire in September, one of the losses of the Revolution.

Fig. 7. Trinity Church, the second building

In 1790, seven years after the end of the war, the second Trinity was completed, one of the few church buildings of the period designed in at least a partly Gothic style. But because it was built so poorly that heavy snows badly damaged its roof in 1839, the structure was torn down.

Fig. 8. Trinity Church, the third building

The present building was completed in 1846, designed by Richard Upjohn, whose Church of the Ascension on lower Fifth Avenue had been completed five years earlier. Although this third Trinity was built in the Gothic style to identify it with the religious period of the Middle Ages, the building was faced with brownstone. This was a controversial choice of materials because until then the stone had been used chiefly for trim; critics considered brownstone too common for such an important building. Two hundred eighty-four feet high, Trinity's spire made the church the tallest structure in New York until the New York tower of the Brooklyn Bridge was completed in 1876, and the tallest building in America until the New York World building was erected in 1890. Nineteenth-century tourists climbed the church steeple to have a good view of New York.

2. *Trinity Churchyard*

Laid out for the first building on the site, Trinity Churchyard is in the simple English style, with neat, curved walks. It contains one gothic structure, considered by some to be America's first monument to its unknown soldiers--the large, blackened Martyr's monument along the north fence. This monument was erected in 1852 to memorialize prisoners of war in the Revolution who are buried nearby, many of whom died in the old Sugar House on Liberty Street.

The north yard also contains a large white cross, in the style of English roadside crosses, a gift to the church in 1914 by Caroline Astor Wilson in memory of her mother, "the" Mrs. Astor. Another member of the family donated the three huge sets of bronze front doors.

1,186 people are buried in the churchyard, most of them unknown today; another 90 private family vaults are within the church. The oldest grave belongs to Richard Churcher, who died at age 5 in 1681. That his grave predates the first church by 17 years indicates that at least part of the land was a graveyard in the earliest Colonial days.

The tombstones tell of sadness in old New York. Many are for children who died at two months, one year, three years. Illnesses at the time--influenza, pneumonia--killed many; there were also plagues--smallpox, cholera, yellow fever. In July through October, the worst months for disease, whoever could afford to do so would escape the crowded downtown neighborhoods for the country--then meaning Greenwich Village or Harlem.

Some stones suggest long life. If a man escaped the worst childhood diseases and shipwrecks and war, he might live a long time. (The short life-expectancy did not mean that few lived beyond their 40s, but that the great amount of infant mortality lowered the average.) In the north yard is the grave of William Bradford, who died in 1752 at age 92. He was the only printer in Manhattan for many years beginning in 1693, and in 1725 began the *New-York Gazette,* New York's first newspaper.

Many renowned people are buried at Trinity, especially heroes of the founding of the Nation. Among them, in the north yard, is Francis Lewis. In addition to giving his name to a boulevard in Queens, he was one of the wealthy merchants who risked their lives and fortunes by signing the Declaration of Independence. He is the only signer buried in Manhattan.

During the Revolution his house in Whitestone, Queens was plundered and his valuable library destroyed.

Lewis represents the devastation that the war brought to families. Although his wife was imprisoned and so badly treated for several months that she soon died, their daughter secretly married a British officer.

In the south yard is the grave of Captain James Lawrence, commander of the ship *Chesapeake,* whose famous dying words in the War of 1812 were "Don't Give Up The Ship." As seems typical with heroes' wives, his wife long survived him. Buried alongside the commander, Julia Lawrence died fifty-two years after he died at thirty-two. Around his grave are cannon barrels captured between 1812 and 1815 from British ships. Those parts of the cannon bearing the British insignia and the names of the ship from which they were taken are buried so as not to gloat over the defeated enemy.

Robert Fulton's monument is against the Rector Street fence. He was trained as a painter--he studied in France under the American expatriate Benjamin West--and his tombstone bears a copy of a self-portrait. His lasting fame, however, is not as an artist, but as the inventor of the steamboat. The 1807 voyage from New York to Albany of the *Clermont* went

Fig. 9. Robert Fulton

against wind and tide to make the trip in record time. And the steam engine, giving power to other tools, such as the printing press, brought industrialization to the cities. Although years earlier John Fitch and others had tried to promote and get backers for the steam engine, it was Fulton who was popularly considered the inventor of the steamboat because he was the first to prove the invention commercially successful in American waters. He had the backing of the

Fig. 10. *Clermont.*

powerful Livingston family. Married to Harriet Livingston--the *Clermont* was named for the Livingston estate in upstate New York--he is buried not beneath this marker but within Trinity Church in the Livingston vault.

Next to Fulton's monument is the grave of Alexander Hamilton. An aide to Washington in the Revolution and first Secretary of the Treasury, Hamilton helped found the first two banks in the state--the Bank of New York (1783) and the Bank of the United States (1792)--as well as the United States Coast Guard (1790) and the New York *Evening Post* (1801.) But Aaron Burr, long his rival, challenged

Hamilton to the famous duel at Weehawken Heights, across the Hudson from West Thirtieth Street. Hamilton was mortally wounded. He died the next day and was buried in Trinity Yard two days later. Two years after his death at just 47, words of adulation were put on his stone. His wife Elizabeth

Fig. 11. The Duel between Burr and Hamilton

Schuyler Hamilton lived another 50 years and is buried next to him.

The native lands of many of the people buried here give some indication of the composition of Manhattan at this time. William

Bradford was from "Old England," Albert Gallatin from Switzerland, Francis Lewis from Wales, and Alexander Hamilton from the West Indies.

3. View from Broadway and Wall Street

Bishop's Crook Lamp

The street lamp in front of Trinity is a "Bishop's Crook Lamp," named for its shape. Its design is a result of the "City Beautiful" movement inspired by the 1893 World's Columbian Exposition in Chicago. The lamp is one of some thirty that remain in New York.

Woolworth Building

With a crown at its peak, the Woolworth Building a few blocks up the west side of Broadway was the tallest building in the world for sixteen years. When it was completed in 1913, it eclipsed the Metropolitan Life Insurance Building at 23rd Street, and in 1929 was itself eclipsed by the Chrysler Building.

Eight-hundred feet tall, with ceilings eleven-to-twenty feet high, the Woolworth Building has only sixty floors, fewer that the eighty a skyscraper with ceilings of modern height might have. F.W. Woolworth wanted the tallest building for his corporate headquarters, chiefly as a huge advertisement for his 5-and-10-cent stores. Since he disliked buying on credit, he paid for this "Cathedral of Commerce" with $13.5 million in cash. Its Gothic cathedral style was chosen more for its picturesqueness than for its religious associations. And picturesque it is. Statues grace the facade; the lobby contains a glass mosaic ceiling; gold leaf covers richly decorated balconies and iron cornices. Most humourously, the lobby includes corbels of the renting agent closing a

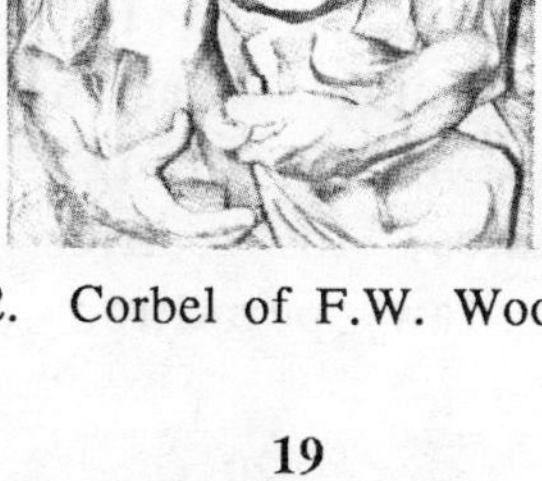

Fig. 12. Corbel of F.W. Woolworth

deal, the architect Cass Gilbert with a miniature model of the building, and F.W. Woolworth counting his nickels and dimes.

The executive offices are on the 24th floor, where the founder's marble-lined offices are still in use.

A four-year restoration begun in 1975 cleaned the entire facade and replaced one fifth of the building's terra cotta surface, all of its 2,843 windows, and many of its architectural details.

Equitable Building, 120 Broadway

This high building on the east side of Broadway had an important effect on further building in New York. Going straight up for its full forty stories with all floors having about the same area, the building interferes with light on the street. To protect pedestrians from such effects by future buildings, in 1916, the year after the Equitable was built, the city passed the first zoning law in the United States, to restrict height and bulk. The law permitted a maximum floor area of twelve times the site's area, as against the Equitable's floor area of almost thirty times.

4. Irving Trust Co., 1 Wall Street

A wonderful Art Deco building completed in 1932, this structure contains an especially impressive lobby with mosaics of red and gold. Coincidentally, Washington Irving, after whom the bank was named in the mid-Nineteenth Century, in 1808 briefly clerked in his brother's law office on the site.

5. New Street

Going down Wall Street you pass what looks like an alley called New Street. The street is hardly new. The name was bestowed in 1674 because the street was the first in this part of town laid out by the new English government.

6. Federal Hall National Memorial

(orginally United States Custom House 1842-62; Sub-Treasury Building 1862-1920,)

28 Wall St., Corner of Nassau

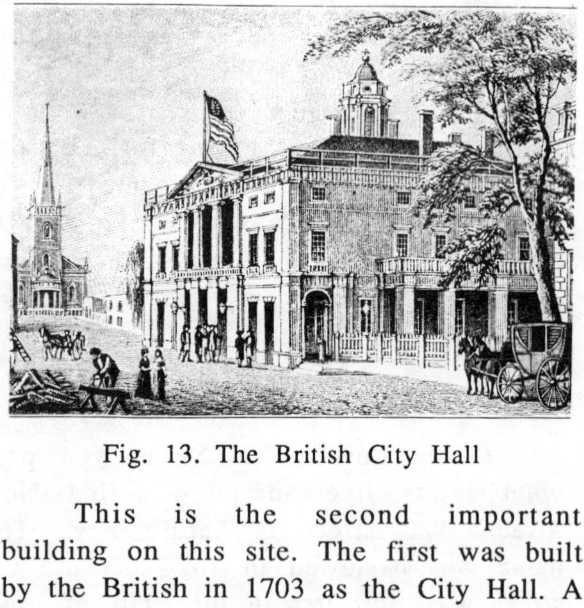

Fig. 13. The British City Hall

This is the second important building on this site. The first was built by the British in 1703 as the City Hall. A two-story, red-brick structure, with tall chimneys, a cupola on the roof, and an arcade above the street, it had rooms for the Governor's Council and the New York Assembly. It had court rooms, a library, offices, a jail in the garret, and a dungeon in the cellar. The jail housed

John Peter Zenger, the German immigrant publisher of the *New York Weekly Journal,* for nine months in 1735 because he had criticized the Royal Governor William Cosby, his Council, and his New York friends. Zenger was jailed until Catherine Zenger, his wife, arranged for the best-known attorney in America, Andrew Hamilton, to come from Philadelphia to defend her husband. Thirty years later the building was again the site of opposition to British leadership when at the Stamp Act Congress, represenlives of nine out of the thirteen Colonies met to protest the onerous stamp tax.

Fig. 14. Washington's Inauguration

To prepare the structure for an inauguration after the Revolution, the old City Hall was remodeled by the man who would later design Washington, D.C., Major Pierre Charles L'Enfant. On April 30, 1789, on the second-floor open-air balcony of the building then called Federal Hall, his hand on a Bible borrowed at the last minute from a nearby Masonic Lodge,

Fig. 15. Unveiling Ward's Statue of Washington in Wall Street

George Washington became the first President of the new United States. The streets below were jammed with cheering spectators. Where the President took the oath of office, today stands a statue of Washington, sculpted by the prolific John Quincy Adams Ward and erected on November 26, 1883, the centennial of the British evacuation.

The building survived the inauguration by 23 years. It ceased being the City Hall in 1812 when the structure still used for that purpose was completed. After the original had been sold for salvage, a new building erected on part of the property served from 1812 to 1816 as The Kirk and Eastburn Bookstore.

It was replaced by the present building, made of stone to be as fireproof as possible. Looking very much like the Parthenon, it is in the Greek Revival style. It was designed in 1835 by Ithiel Towne and Alexander Jackson Davis, leaders of the Greek Revival in New York, and designers of the elegant row of houses on the north side of Washington Square. This style was popular in New York from 1828 to the middle 1840s because the wars with England in 1776 and in 1812 removed Americans from British architectural models, while the Greek wars for independence in the 1820s brought Americans closer to ancient Greek prototypes. But the style died out in the mid-1840s--ideologically because the new mood of Abolitionism reminded Americans that the ancient Greeks had kept slaves, and practically because a building surrounded by columns could not easily be enlarged.

Fig. 16. Federal Hall

This building has served many functions. From 1842 to 1862, it was the United States Custom House; from 1862 to 1920 it was a branch of the independent Treasury system; from 1920 it held offices for several government organizations. It became a museum in 1940, when the Federal Hall Memorial Association installed historical exhibits removed from the George Washington Pavilion of the New York World's Fair. In 1955 it was established as a national historical memorial, administered by the National Park Service of the United States Department of the Interior. Its magnificent rotunda makes for one of the great interior spaces in New York. The memorial contains dioramas depicting Washington's inauguration and many historical exhibits including Washington's homespun brown suit in which he took the oath of office.

7. Morgan Guaranty Trust Co., formerly J.P. Morgan & Co., 23 Wall Street

Austere and elegant, the facade of the building on the southeast corner of Wall and Broad streets bears no name. When the building was erected in 1913, no name was needed: all passers by were supposed to know that this was the famous bank of J.P. Morgan, epitome of American capitalism. Its Wall Street side contains pock marks in the stone--the remains of a disaster here on September 16, 1920. It was a weekday lunch hour when, amid the thousands of office workers passing on the street, a driver parked his horse-drawn cart next to the bank and disappeared. The cart, filled with dynamite, exploded, injuring 400 people and killing 33 people and the horse.

One of the dead was the owner of Sweet's Restaurant, who was identifiable only by the ring still attached to a finger. The driver was never found, but it was believed that he had been an anarchist interested in damaging Morgan and his bank. J.P. Morgan, Jr. himself was in Scotland at the time and only one person within the bank was injured, but the scars in the side of the building remain to remind passersby of one of the great physical disasters of the area.

The corner building now serves as an impressive symbol rather than functioning offices, according to Paul Goldberger, architecture critic of the *New York Times,* since much of the work of the bank is done in "anonymous buildings" next door. Morgan Guaranty Trust Company will soon be moving into its new headquarters building, now under construction one block east on Wall

Street.

8. 40 Wall Street, orginally the Bank of the Manhattan Co.

Planned as the tallest building in the world, the Bank of the Manhattan Company was being completed in 1929, when the architect of the Chrysler Building, being erected at the same time, added a high tower to his plan. The tower made the Chrysler Building rather that the Wall Street bank the world's tallest.

9. The Bank of New York, 48 Wall Street

The Bank of New York, founded by Alexander Hamilton 110 days after the British evacuated the Colonies, is the oldest bank in New York City. The present building, built between 1927 and 1928, is the bank's third home on this site since 1798. The 1797 cornerstone is at the west end of the building.

10. Citibank, 55 Wall St.

Fig. 17. Citibank, Orig.: Merchant's Exchange (3 stories with a large dome) 1836-42 Isaiah Rogers; used as U.S. Customs House between 1863 and 1899. Remodeled with second tier of three stories added for National City Bank (Citibank) in 1907 by McKim, Mead and White.

The lower four-story portico was built in 1836-42 to house the Merchants' Exchange. Each of the massive columns is a single piece of stone, brought by ship from a Quincy, Massachusetts quarry to the foot of Wall Street, there to be pulled by many horses to this site. After a period of use from 1863 to 1899 as the United States Custom House, the building was bought in 1907 by First National City Bank, which had the renowned architectural firm of McKim, Mead and White remodel it by adding the upper tier of four stories.

11. New York Stock Exchange 8 Broad Street

Fig 18. Scene in the Gold Room, 1869

The lower building of the Exchange was designed in the neo-Renaissance style by George B. Post and erected in 1903, replacing a building created for the exchange in 1865. The corner building was designed by Trowbridge and Livingston to add more working room during the bull market of 1923. A buttonwood tree has been planted on the Broad Street side to commemorate a similar tree under which the first New York Stock Exchange was established in 1792 at Wall and William Streets. The Stock Exchange grew out of a need to create a formal market place to handle $80 million in bonds which had been issued by Congress in 1789 and 1790 to pay the Revolutionary War Debts.

Fig. 19. New York Stock Exchange

Especially striking is the high-relief pediment named "Integrity

Protecting the Works of Man," depicting the central figure blessing the industries and activities that create American capital, as represented by a farmer, a mechanic, and a prospector. Its creator was J.Q.A. Ward, sculptor of the statue of Washington across the street. But the pediment is not the original. To quote the *AIA Guide to New York City,* "The orginal mythological figures of the pediment became so deteriorated that their stone was replaced with sheet metal, secretively, so that the public would not know that any facet of the Stock Exchange was vulnerable."

12. Broad Street

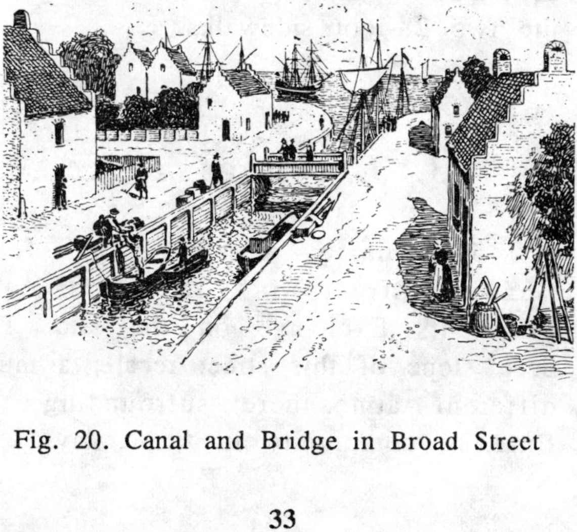

Fig. 20. Canal and Bridge in Broad Street

When the Dutch first arrived in 1624, at the foot of the island they found a half-block long inlet of the sea. Used to canals in Holland, the colonists extended this inlet into a canal up what is now Broad Street as far north as Exchange Place. Boats used the canal. Pedestrians crossed it on footbridges or walked next to it on sidewalks. But the canal became terribly polluted because many New Yorkers habitually threw their garbage into it. In 1676, after twelve years of rule by the English, who had little tradition of canals, the waterway was filled in with fresh dirt to form Broad Street. The street was appropriately named: its 72-foot width contains the old sixteen-foot canal and the two 28-foot sidewalks.

13. Exchange Place

The name was changed from Garden Street in 1827 for the Merchants Exchange on the site. The deep slope of this street recalls a much different atmosphere surrounding the financial community in those days. In the Seventeenth Century, Broad Street bankers and brokers feared being hit by the local children who raced down this hill on sleds.

14. 50 Broadway

An earlier building in this location was the first skyscraper in New York. The owner of the long, narrow site in 1889 was afraid that he could not get much rental income if he built a standard brick structure. Because the walls would have to be thick to support the building, offices would be too small for much profit. So instead of using brick, he used the new steel girders--today's steel-cage construction. The result, called the Tower Building, was not tall, just eleven stories high. But it was taller than any other office building in town and narrower that any other building of relative height. Because many people were sure it would collapse, the designer Bradford L. Gilbert put his own office on the top floor to show his confidence. Soon the success of the building caused its demotition: if builders could erect an eleven-story structure, even more profit could be made from a higher building. The race was on for the tallest building in America. In the next 24 years six New York buildings successively won the title.

15. Cunard Building 25 Broadway

At the cross streets looking west on lower Broadway, one can see the Hudson River, recalling a time when the river was very much part of city life. The wealthiest families in town got their income from the sea, whether as merchants, shipowners, or privateers. Because of its proximity to the sea, lower Broadway has traditionally housed steamship companies. The Cunard Building was erected in 1921 to house the company that ran the fastest, most luxurious liners in the world. First-class tickets were sold in the magnificent Great Hall, an octagon shaped room 185 feet long and 74 feet wide. With a dome 65 feet above the floor over the central section, it is one of the great open interior spaces in New York. When Cunard left the building in 1976, a poor renovation was done to enable the United States Post Office to use the palatially domed Great Hall.

16. Bowling Green

Many periods of Manhattan history converge on the site of Bowling Green. During the Dutch period, soldiers from adjoining Fort Amsterdam used the site for marching drill, and colonists bought and sold their cattle at the weekly market. During the English period, British soldiers and others used it for playing the games of bowls--something like our bowling. The green became the city's first park in 1733 when three men leased it for public use from the city, for the nominal sum of one peppercorn a year.

In the years leading to the Revolution, here the colonists expressed their pleasure or displeasure with the ruling British. When the Stamp Act was passed in England in the 1760s, it taxed for the first time such items in New York as newspapers, legal documents, even playing cards. The colonists felt the charge to be so onerous that when Parliament repealed it in 1770, to show their gratitude New Yorkers erected the largest statue yet in America, a larger-than-life-size equestrian of George III

Fig. 21. Removing the Statue of George III (in dress of the 1840's)

dressed as a Roman emperor, made of lead and covered with gold leaf. They put it in Bowling Green in 1770 and the next year erected an iron fence with gold-plated crowns to protect it. But relations between England and the

Colonies deteriorated. When the Declaration of Independence was read in front of City Hall, on July 9, 1776, an angry mob marched to Bowling Green and tore down its symbols of British monarchy. The statue and crowns were taken from there to Litchfield, Connecticut, to be melted into bullets for the war.

Some pieces of the statue--the horse's tail, for example--were recently found near Wilton, Connecticut, and can now be seen at the New-York Historical Society. Although the crowns removed in 1776 were replaced by graceful lamps after the Revolution, these lamps have since disappeared. The fence around the green today is the same one erected over two hundred years ago.

After the Revolution some of the city's wealthiest families lived at the foot of Broadway and fattened their private livestock on the park grass.

Bowling Green was the scene of great jubilation in 1842. After many epidemics and fires, the city finally received a plentiful supply of good water when the Croton River of Westchester was diverted into New York City plumbing. In a town with poor water for so long that during the Revolution horses from Philadelphia were reportedly loathe to drink New York water, where New Yorkers had used public well water too dirty to drink for putting out fires and citizens had commonly caught rain water in cisterns for washing clothes, three fountains were built to celebrate the new profusion of clean water--one in Union Square Park, one in City Hall Park, the third in Bowling Green.

When the City renovated Bowling Green in the 1970s, many periods of its history were wisely recalled. The street between the Green and the Custom House was closed to traffic and paved with Belgian blocks to make it more of a unit with the Custom House, reminiscent of when the Dutch soldiers marched out of the fort and the soldiers came from the fort to bowl on the Green. The subway station entrance was sunk out of sight so that it would not intrude into the view of the Green. And a fountain was installed reminiscent of the 1842 Croton celebration.

17. The United States Custom House

Fig. 22. The Fort

On the site of forts from Fort Amsterdam to Fort George, the United States Custom House was erected in 1907. It was designed by Cass Gilbert, who six years later would complete the Woolworth Building a few blocks up Broadway. The building that housed the Custom Service of the New York Port was properly grand: before the income tax was insituted in 1916, customs duty provided the bulk of income to the Federal Government, and New York was the largest port.

The building is considered the finest example in New York of the Beaux-Arts style. In this style the architecture conveys the function of the building--here grand steps going to the main door clearly show the entrance. A Beaux-Arts building employs painting and sculpture as part of the architectural design, and the second-floor rotunda includes a wonderful series of WPA-sponsored paintings by Reginald Marsh that depict the various stages of the landing of a steamship in the Port of New York, including a panel showing reporters interviewing a debarking Greta Garbo.

The front facade contains two sets of figures. The statues at the base, called the Four Continents, were sculpted by Daniel Chester French, best known for his seated Lincoln at the Lincoln Memorial in Washington, D.C.

At either end are what were then considered the less important continents. The statue at the right represents Africa. She seems to be sleeping deeply, with one arm resting on a sphinx, the other on a lion. The statue at the left represents Asia. The iconlike figure is rapt in meditation and is surrounded by figures in prayer; she holds a small figure of Buddha. Amid these images of spirituality are also signs of oppression--a tiger glares into her face, while skulls lie under her feet.

To the right of the door is Europe, alert and solemn. Enthroned and with an arm resting on a globe, she shows the satisfaction of an established empire. The open book, the globe, and the ship's prow stand for her exploits. She is surrounded by such symbols representing the past as a frieze from the Parthenon.

To the left of the door, in contrast, is America--the embodiment of energy. Although some symbols convey the country the first European settlers found--the Aztec image under her foot, the bunch of cornstalks on her lap, and the Indian peering over her shoulder--she looks eagerly to the future. She holds the torch of liberty and protects the youth at her side, who sets a winged wheel in motion to symbolize progress.

The set of statues at the roof was done just before World War I. It represents twelve great commercial centers of the world--including Phoenicia, Genoa, Holland, and Portugal. The third from the end on the right is a Germanic, Teutonic statue; the incongruous inscription "Belgium" on the shield reveals that in that anti-German pre-World War I period, it was easier to give an innocuous label to the Germanic image than to remove the statue.

The Custom Department moved from this building to the World Trade Center in 1973; the Post Office moved from the first floor to the Cunard Building in 1977. The magnificent structure has been empty since that time.

18. 26 Broadway, formerly the Standard Oil Building

Just to the east of Bowling Green is 26 Broadway. The architects of the 42nd Street Library (1911) Carrere and Hastings designed this building (1922) in a most unusual style: its top and bottom are treated as two separate elements. The upper portion is aligned with the midtown skyline, while, at a completely different angle, its base follows the gentle curve of the street. The oil lamp at the peak of the building is appropriate: for many years the building was the New York headquarters of Standard Oil, its home throughout the antitrust suit against it in the beginning of this century, which broke the giant company into the Socony and Mobil Oil Companies. In 1956 Socony Mobil left this building for its new headquarters on 42nd Street.

19. Battery Park

Near the rocks called Kapsee, where Indians had landed on their trips from Brooklyn, the British kept a battery of guns from 1683 to 1687 to protect the harbor. Named for this battery, the present 22-acre park was created atop the rocks after the

Fig. 23. The Battery in 1746

Revolution. Landfill for its creation came from the rubble that had been Fort George, on the site of the present Custom House.

20. Netherlands Memorial Flagpole in Battery Park

With its inscription in English and Dutch, this pole was a gift from the Dutch Government to commemorate the famous purchase of the island from the Indians. This 1626 sale has long been considered slightly humorous--the whole island for just $24. But it was a bad bargain because the agreement had different meanings to the participants. The Dutch Governor Peter

Fig. 24. The Purchase of Manhattan Island

Minuit bought the land as the sole property of the Dutch West India Co. But because the Indians had no concept of private ownership of land, they were selling the right to the Dutch just to share the land. In later years when the Indians tried to remain on the land, or in one instance when an Indian woman picked a peach from a Dutch orchard, many Indians and Europeans were killed.

21. Castle Clinton National Monument, the building occupying the Battery

South of the flagpole along the water's edge is Castle Clinton. Like Bowling Green, it has participated in many periods of New York history.

Originally called the West Battery, the structure was built as a fort in 1807 in 35 feet of water, 200 feet from the shoreline. Its purpose was to defend the island against the British at a time of increasing tension between

Fig. 25. DeWitt Clinton

the United States and England, which eventually broke out into the War of

1812. During the war New York was not invaded as Washington, D.C. was, possibly because of its protection by such forts as this. The structure was renamed Fort Clinton in 1815 after the former mayor of New York City and later governor of New York State, DeWitt Clinton.

In 1824, the year after the Federal Government ceded the fort to New York City, the structure was joined to the land by a causeway, and the city began leasing it as a place of public entertainment. From then until 1851 it was a concert hall called Castle Garden. Something like the Madison Square Garden of the time, it housed "Fanciful Gardens," band concerts, fireworks, an occasional balloon ascension, and demonstrations of the latest scientific achievements. Its most celebrated moment of this period came in 1850 with the arrival of soprano Jenny Lind, the "Swedish Nightingale," skillfully promoted by her manager P.T. Barnum. By the time she arrived in New York, he had so excited the public that they were willing to bid on tickets for her first concert. Over 6,000 people paid the exorbitant fee of at least $3 for a seat. A hatmaker named Genin bid $225 for the first seat. Barnum generated excitement by setting up controversy--writing to the newspapers that Lind was the most wonderful creature the world had known, then writing in anonymously that Lind was greatly overrated. He had her donate proceeds of several concerts to charities. She did so well that she thought she, no longer needed Barnum--and flopped.

Fig. 26. Jenny Lind at Castle Garden

So many immigrants came to New York Port from Ireland and Germany in the 1840s and '50s that by 1850 most of the city was foreign-born. In 1855 the State began using Castle Clinton as the first immigrant landing station in New York to process entering immigrants in a more orderly fashion. For the first time, bewildered immigrants were protected from the unsavory characters who had frequented the docks to prey on them. Here generally reliable information about boarding houses, travel routes, and fares could be got. Newcomers could find jobs, medical help, and an honest currency exchange.

Fig. 27. Immigrants

Over eight million people came through its gates, more that two-third of the immigrants to the United States in this period. Rather helpless and often unfamiliar with English and the ways of their new country, the new immigrants were still taken advantage of, especially by their compatriots who had arrived earlier. For that reason the immigrant landing office moved from Castle Garden to the more protectable barge office at the battery in 1890, then in 1892 to Ellis Island.

Castle Clinton became a new kind of center. In 1896, remodeled by the architectural firm of McKim, Mead and White, it was turned into the extremely popular New York City Aquarium. It was a great tourist attraction until 1941, by which time some 90 million people had visited it. Then for a combination of reasons, including pollution of the harbor water and interference with the approaches to the Brooklyn-Battery Tunnel, the Aquarium was moved to Coney Island.

In response to the popular outcry against the demolition of the building, in 1946 the Federal Government established Castle Clinton as a National Historical Monument. Following restoration by the National Park Service, it reopened in 1975 in time for the Bicentennial. But unlike the restoration of Bowling Green, it was restored not to its many lives as concert hall, immigrant landing station, or aquarium--only to its earliest period as fort. It currently includes pictures of the fort's past life, a sparsely-furnished officer's quarters--and the ticket sales booth for the Liberty Island ferryboat.

22. Admiral George Dewey Promenade

Because this tip of Manhattan at the water's edge is one of the coolest parts of the island, it was popular for summer promenades and today is crowded on a hot summer day. Many New Yorkers promenaded here, even the transvestite governor Edward Hyde, Lord Cornbury, who was stopped by a constable here in 1705 for dressing in women's clothes.

The view from the promenade is spectacular. Brooklyn Heights is at left. Next are three islands. Governor's Island has served as a race track and summer resort, a prison for prisoners of war, and a troop embarkation point: Castle William on the island guarded New York Harbor during the War of

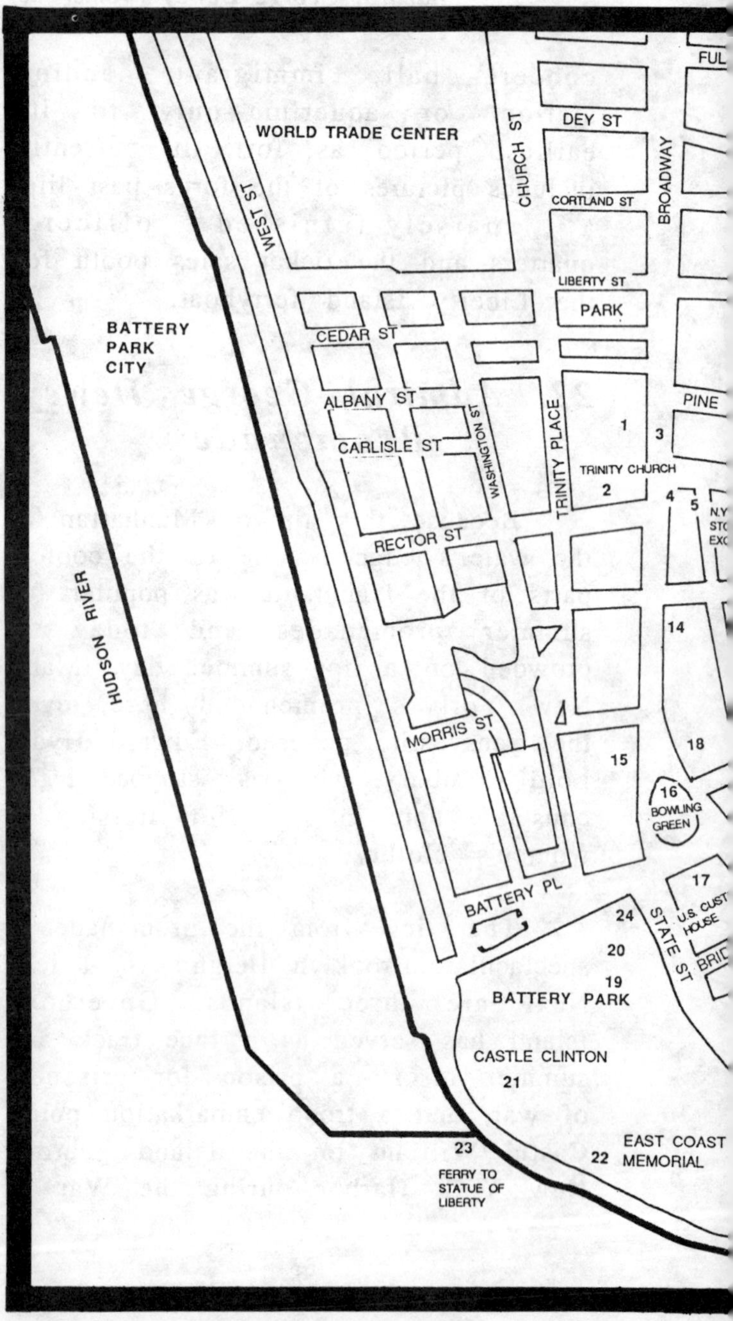
FUL
WORLD TRADE CENTER
CHURCH ST
DEY ST
BROADWAY
CORTLAND ST
WEST ST
LIBERTY ST
PARK
BATTERY
PARK
CITY
CEDAR ST
ALBANY ST
PINE
WASHINGTON ST
TRINITY PLACE
1
3
CARLISLE ST
TRINITY CHURCH
2
4
5
N.Y
STO
EXC
RECTOR ST
HUDSON RIVER
14
MORRIS ST
18
15
16
BOWLING
GREEN
17
BATTERY PL
24
STATE ST
U.S. CUST
HOUSE
20
BRID
19
BATTERY PARK
CASTLE CLINTON
21
23
EAST COAST
22 MEMORIAL
FERRY TO
STATUE OF
LIBERTY

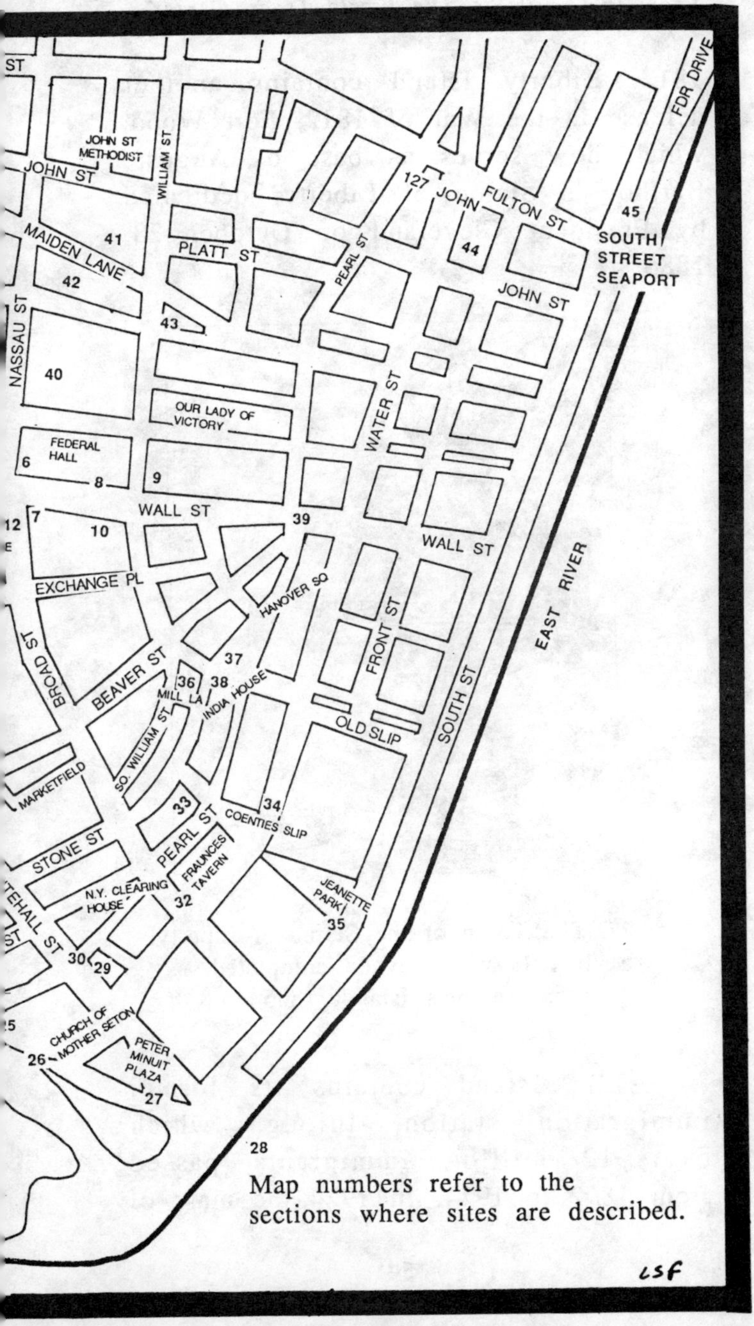

Map numbers refer to the sections where sites are described.

1812. Liberty Island contains another defense in the War of 1812, Fort Wood, which now serves as base of Auguste Bartholdi's Statue of Liberty, dedicated by President Cleveland on October 28, 1886.

Fig. 28. The Torch of the Statue of Liberty,
as it will appear when completed
on Bedloe's Island, 1885

Ellis Island contains its former immigration station, through which over 12 million immigrants passed from 1892 to 1924. In 1924 the mass of immigration ended because of the institution of immigration quotas. Under this system, immigrants were inspected in their country of origin. From 1924 to 1954 Ellis was used for deportation, for use by the Coast Guard, and for the detention of enemy aliens. It is now being restored as a museum.

23. Pier A, Battery Park, adjacent to Castle Clinton

The oldest pier remaining in New York, this landmark was built in 1886 for the City's Department of Docks and Harbor Police. It is now used as the headquarters of the Fire Department's Marine Division. The clock tower installed in 1919 to memorialize the war dead of World War I rings ship's bells every half hour.

24. Subway Kiosk, State Street near Battery Place

Modeled after summerhouses of ancient Persia and Turkey, this Bowling Green station is one of a pair in Manhattan in the original 1904-05 design. Designed by the architectural firm of Heins and LaFarge, it is now used as the Battery Park Control House.

25. 17 State Street

On this site from 1969 to 1986 was the Seamen's Church Institute. Since 1834 the organization has served to improve the treatment of merchant seamen entering the Port of New York.

Fig. 29. The Floating Church of Our Saviour, 1870-1910

Herman Melville was born in 1819 on the part of this site known a 6 Pearl Street. In his youth he worked on a ship that sailed out of the South Street Seaport.

Fig. 30. Herman Melville

26. Rectory of the Shrine of Saint Mother Elizabeth Seton, (originally the James Watson House,) 7 State Street

The rectory is a shrine to a woman who converted to Catholicism after her husband's death, founded the first order of nuns in the United States, (the American Sisters of Charity,) and established the American parochial school system. Mother Seton's canonization in 1974 made her the first American-born saint. As an Episcopalian, Elizabeth Bayley Seton (1774-1821) had lived with her family on the site of the Church of Our Lady of the Rosary adjoining the shrine.

The building in which the rectory is housed, once called the James Watson House, is the last survivor of a row of eight elegant Federal-style homes built when State Street was one of New York's finest addresses. The right side of the house was built two-windows wide in 1793 in the Georgian style. The left side was added in 1806 in the Federal style. Its curved porch is attributed to architect John McComb, Jr. The attenuated columns, characteristic of the Federal style, were made from ships' masts. This nautical association is especially appropriate here because Watson was a "peep o'day" boy, a shipowner so eager for news of the arrival of his ships that at the first "peep o'day" he was out with his spyglass to see if his employee on Staten Island was signaling the arrival at the Narrows of Watson's ship.

The brickwork, which looks like long bricks alternating with short bricks, is actually the side of one brick alternating with the head of the next, a style called Flemish Bond, popularly used in New York prior to 1835.

27. Peter Minuit Plaza

This plaza was named for the first governor of New Amsterdam, the Huguenot Peter Minuit, who in 1626 bought the island for $24 in trinkets from the Canarsie Indians on behalf of the Dutch West India Co.

The bronze plaque at the base of the plaza flagpole was mounted by New York State in 1954 to commemorate the three-hundredth anniversary of the arrival of the first Jews to Manhattan. They came from Brazil. Although Recife in northern Brazil was run by the Dutch West India Co. and as such was a haven for Jews expelled in the 1490s from Spain and Portugal, in 1654 the Portuguese conquered Recife. All who had been loyal to the Dutch, expecially the Jews, were forced to leave quickly. On their way back to Amsterdam, six men and women and seventeen children were shipwrecked and taken by pirates, but finally their French ship, the *St. Charles,* dropped them at the nearest Dutch colony, New Amsterdam. To raise money for their passage, the Jews' personal possessions were auctioned. When the sum realized was too little, two of the immigrants were jailed as hostages until the remaining payment could be received from relatives in Amsterdam.

28. The Old South Brooklyn Ferry Piers, 11 South Street

Fig. 31. Ferry to Brooklyn

On the site of the old Dutch Schreier's ("Crier's") Hoek, the place of departure during the Dutch period of Manhattan, is the last of the ferry terminal buildings on the East River. Erected in 1909, it closed in 1938, after almost thirty years of docking

Brooklyn ferries. The piers are now used for the Coast Guard ferry to Governor's Island.

29. The New York Health & Racquet Club, 39 Whitehall Street

This is a 1986 structural concrete building placed on top of an iron-framed building 100 years older. Until 1986 here stood the United States Army Building. With "U.S. Army" and "1886" incised on its facade, this building was where thousands of recruits were "injected, inspected, detected and selected" to become soldiers for duty on the American prairies, in the European forests, Pacific islands, African deserts, and finally, Vietnam. After here being the focus of some of the angriest anti-Vietnam war demonstrations of the 1960s, the Army left the building in 1972. In 1978 the structure was bought by the New York Health and Racquet Club, which provides its members with quite a different type of exercise than that offered to the previous inductees.

30. Whitehall Street

This street housed Governor Stuyvesant's 2-1/2 story white-brick town house, to which he commuted from his farm near the Bowery. Whitehall Street is named for this white hall, a deprecating term given to the building by the English Governor Dongan, who compared it sarcastically to what was then the English royal palace, Whitehall.

Fig. 32. The Mansion of Peter Stuyvesant at the south side of Pearl Street

31. Fires

Fig. 33. Old Fire Engine

On September 21, 1776, a terrible fire broke out first in a wooden house near the Whitehall ferry slip, and then at five or six other distant places. Most of the city's fire engines had been sabotaged, hoses had been cut, bucket handles had been removed--clearly the fire had been set. One quarter of the city was destroyed by the fire, 500 to 1000 homes. Historians seem unsure whether the instigators were the British trying to weaken the resolve of the Americans by destroying much of a major city, or the patriots themselves trying to lay waste the island the

British were sure to occupy.

A second terrible fire broke out, on a bitterly cold day in December 1835. This was apparently an accident. Nevertheless, 674 buildings were lost on the twenty acres involved--from Wall Street to Coenties Slip, from Broad Street to the East River. Only gunpowder brought by boat from the Brooklyn Navy Yard stopped the spread

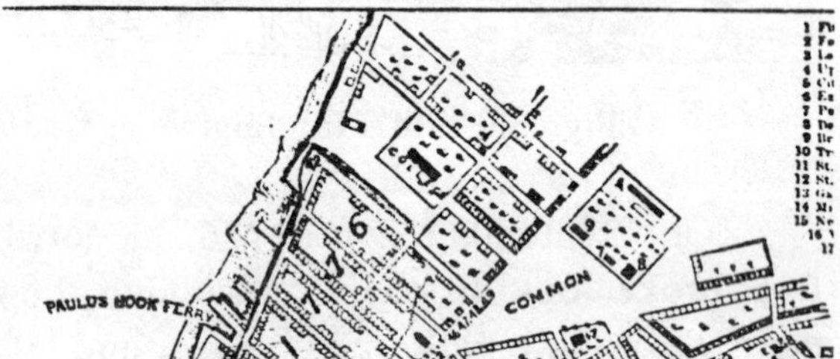

Fig. 34. Map of the fire of 1776

of the flames. This fire was the immediate impetus to providing the city with a reliable supply of water. Within seven years, forty miles of pipes carried Croton River water through underground aqueducts to the Harlem River. Pipes crossed the river at High Bridge. The project cost $12 million. It at once gave water to 6000 homes, and permitted the installation of New York's first fire hydrants.

Fig. 35. Map of the Fire of 1835

32. *Fraunces Tavern*

Only 40 percent of this building remains from the original structure built in 1719 by the wealthy merchant Etienne, or Stephen, Delancey. When he built the house, it was at the edge of the East River near the merchant's docked ships. A garden surrounded the house, and trees led from it almost to the river's edge. When landfill pushed the river out a block, Delancey sold the structure in 1730 and moved to an uptown estate, located where Delancey Street on the Lower East Side is today.

Fig. 36. Fraunces Tavern

The original building passed from one hand to another, until in 1763 it came to be the property of a West Indian innkeeper. Samuel Fraunces established in the building an ordinary called The Sign of the Queen Charlotte, later known as the Queen's Head, a popular meeting place for the revolution-fomenting Sons of Liberty.

The most memorable incident in the tavern took place on December 4, 1783. Just nine days after the British evacuation, Washington here bade a tearful farewell to the generals who had helped him win the war.

The building changed. In 1837 the interior was completely burned out. In 1852 the roof and east end were destroyed by fire. It became a rooming house and tavern to serve the needs of waterfront denizens. In the Nineteenth Century it acquired two more stories and a flat roof. Most of the brick was replaced by cement. The building became a German rooming-house with a street-floor beer parlor.

In 1907 the Sons of the Revolution restored the building. Because at the time there were few clues as to how it looked when Delancey lived near his ships or when Washington came for dinner, the restoration was built almost from scratch. A "tasteful fabrication" of a representation of a typical Georgian brick townhouse, the tavern is now a museum.

What is possibly even more important than the tavern here is the tavern block, one of the few remaining groups of authentic 1776-1825-era New York warehouses and shipping offices. The buildings on the block were being assembled for demolition for an office building when the private, nonprofit New York City Landmarks Conservancy bought the five buildings along Coenties Slip for conversion into apartments, thus keeping out any developer with designs on the block.

33. Stadt Huys Site, 85 Pearl Street

A tavern on this corner was converted in 1653 to the Dutch City Hall, the Stadt Huys. Next to it was the Lovelace Tavern. In 1698 the Stadt Huys, then City Hall, was deemed unsafe, and the city government moved temporarily into Lovelace's Tavern, while a new City Hall was being built at the head of Broad Street. Three hundred twenty-six years later, before the foundation of the proposed Goldman Sachs headquarters building

Fig. 37. City Hall and Great Dock, 1679

could destroy what remained of the buried history, archeologists conducted a dig. Much was found--four tons in all, especially in the old tavern well--including turkey bones, bits of wood, buttons, coins, apothecary jars, bits of pottery jars, pipe stems, and many clam and oyster shells. The trash tells something of the diet of the early settlers and the terrain that produced the food. Some of the findings, including part of the well and building foundations, can be seen through a plastic covering in the sidewalk. A bronze map of New Amsterdam is in the pavement outside the building's main entrance. This was New York's first instance of New York builders permitting scholars to research a spot before construction had begun.

34. Coenties Slip

A corruption of the name of the local landowner Conraet Ten Eyck, Coenties Slip is one of many slips along the East River--Peck, Old, Catherine, Beekman, Burling, and Pike. The presence of slips suggests both the history of landfill and of river traffic in the area. Landfill widened the island into the East River. Some inlets were kept in the new shoreline to allow boats to slip somewhat inland for easier loading and unloading. With the subsequent decline of shipping in this area, the inlets were filled in. They ceased being slips, except in name only.

From 1878 until it was torn down in 1950, the Third Avenue elevated train made a zigzag turn at Coenties Slip. To accommodate this turn, one building at the Slip was built with its

Pearl Street corner shaved off.

Note the metal stars on the buildings on the south side of the slip. Not mere decorations, they fasten the end of tie rods that go through the building to help stabilize the load-bearing wall.

35. Jeanette Park

Jeanette was not a woman, but a ship that the United States Navy and the New York *Herald* sent in 1881 to explore the Arctic. In the first Jeanette Park on the site, seamen congregated each morning to be assigned work. The present park was built in 1972.

36. Mill Lane

A mill was once on this site. Erected in 1626, its upstairs room was used not only for religious services --for the first Dutch services and from 1660 for Jewish worship--but in 1664 it was used for signing the Dutch surrender to the British. Some street names were slightly different then--today's South William Street was then

Fig. 38. The Mill St. Synagogue

called Mill Street; today's Mill Lane was often called Jews' Alley around 1700 because of the Jewish ghetto in the neighborhood. The first synagogue in North America and the only one in New York from 1730 until 1834, thirty-five feet square and twenty-one feet high to allow for a women's gallery, the Spanish-Portuguese Shearith-Israel stood around the corner with 200 feet on Mill Street. Two of its millstones can be seen today in the present home of its original congregation, at 70th Street and Central Park West.

37. Hanover Square,

the intersection of Hanover, Pearl, Stone and William Sts. with Old Slip

This was the original Printing House Square of New York, where in 1693, at 81 Pearl Street, William Bradford established the first printing press in the colony. Another famous inhabitant of the Square was Captain Kidd, hanged as a pirate though possibly innocent, who lived at 199 Pearl Street. Although named for the family of the British King George, the Square kept its name even after the Revolution.

In 1794 many other Royal names were changed--Queen became an extension of Pearl Street, Princess became part of Beaver Street. Three streets were changed to honor trees--King to Pine, George to Spruce, Little Queen to Cedar. Crown Street was changed to Liberty Street. Hanover Square was altered, too, to become part of Pearl St.--but alone of all the royal name changes, this change did not last.

38. India House,
orginally Hanover Bank, New York Cotton Exchange, 1872-85, and W.R. Grace & Co., 1895-1912, 1 Hanover Square

This is one of the earliest buildings in New York to be covered with brownstone, a material generally used for residences. Completed in 1854, it served first as the Hanover Bank. It housed the Cotton Exchange from 1872 to 1885, and R.W. Grace & Co. from 1885 to 1912. The building is one of the few surviving New York banking houses of the mid-19th Century. It was remodeled in 1924 for India House, the private business club. The club is still private, but Harry's Bar on the lower floor is open to the public.

39. Pearl and Wall Streets

It was here that the water gate out of New Amsterdam went through the wall. If you have taken the tour from the beginning, you have traveled the approximate circumference of New Amsterdam.

Fig. 39. Foot of Wall Street, 1674

Sharing the space with a corn and meal market, at the foot of Wall Street was a slave market from 1709 to 1762, where blacks and Indians were both sold and rented out for the day. Of the 20% of the New Yorkers in 1741 who were black, some were free, working as porters, as longshoremen, or as tavern helpers; some owned property.

Although dwarfed by high buildings, Trinity Church commands

the street, sitting at the head of Wall Street, as it has since the first Trinity was built on the site almost 300 years ago.

40. Chase Manhattan Plaza

West of Pearl Street at Pine are four trees--or at least that is the name of the aluminum and fiberglass sculpture by Jean DuBuffet in the Chase Manhattan Bank Plaza. After World Was II, little building was going on in lower Manhattan. Businesses were moving uptown, and it looked as if midtown would be the only vibrant business section in the next decades. But when David Rockefeller, Chairman of Chase Manhattan Bank, built his corporate headquarters downtown in 1960, construction returned to the area. This is a prototype building in the Plaza Style, by Skidmore, Owings and Merrill, increasing height in exchange for leaving open space around the base of the building.

41. Maiden Lane

The street name recalls a much different view from that visible today. The Dutch named this street for the young women of New Amsterdam who washed their clothes here and laid them out to dry at a small stream that flowed east to the river. The Dutch called the street T'Maagde Paatje, which was translated by the British to Maiden Lane.

Fig. 40. Smit's Vlei

At the foot of Maiden Lane in 1695, a man named Smith established a ferry to the Long Island farming markets. He gave his name to the area. It was called Smith's Valley, or "Vlei," and eventually corrupted into the "fly" market, when the farmers began selling their produce on the site.

42. Federal Reserve Bank of New York, 33 Liberty Street

The 1924 building to the west of Pearl Street is the Federal Reserve Bank of New York, housed in a neo-Renaissance fortress said to be modeled after the Palazzo Strozzi of the 15th Century Florentine banking family. It looks like a fortress. And indeed it is a fortress. In the lowest floor of this bank are more gold bars than anywhere else on earth, over one-third more than in Fort Knox. More than one-quarter of the official monetary gold of the free world is held in safekeeping for many foreign nations, and is partly the basis of their currency. Five floors down, some 76 feet below the street and 50 feet below sea level, this building gives the appearance of a little country jail. The 122 cells house over 12,000 tons of gold, the property of 80 countries and organizations. When one country pays a debt to another, rather than ship gold from country to country, the bullion may be moved from cell to cell. If, for example, France pays Germany a debt of millions of dollars, the gold to back that exchange is moved from the French cell to the German cell. Scales used to weigh the bars are so sensitive that they weigh to the nearest 1/100 of a troy ounce, one-third the weight of a dollar bill.

Some of the gold is kept in America because at certain times of unrest, especially at the outset of World War II, it seemed safer here than in Europe. The gold is stored at the Fed in New York because it is this branch that has the most dealings with foreign nations.

Fig. 41. The Gold Vault at the Federal Reserve Bank

Some functions of the New York Fed are representative of activity in all twelve member banks. Each workday morning, dozens of armored cars line up in front of the building to deposit the excess cash of member banks. As an individual might deposit spare cash into, say, Chemical Bank, so Chemical deposits its cash into this bank. Over 60,000 bills an hour are individually processed in the building. If one is found to be counterfeit, or over one year old, it is shredded and used for landfill or household insulation. A new bill replaces it. The new bill will have a "2," a "B," and, "Federal Reserve Bank of New York" printed on its face, signifying that it was put into circulation in this building rather than in one of the other eleven Federal Reserve banks. The banks also handle transactions between Federal Reserve Districts. If your bank is in the New York district, for example, the bank checks you use to pay bills in other parts of the country are returned to you through a long route. The recipient deposits the check in a local bank; that bank sends the check to its local Federal Reserve Bank; that Fed sends it to the New York Fed, which sends it to your bank, which returns it to you. This physical moving of checks from Fed to Fed is one reason it can take ten days for a check to clear all the stops.

Among the most interesting tours in Lower Manhattan is that given of the Federal Reserve Bank. It is free of charge, but reservations must be made up to one month in advance.

43. Nevelson Plaza

The park contains seven abstract sculptures by Louise Nevelson. The works were anonymously donated, and businesses in the area contributed $200,000 for design, construction, permanent security, and maintenance of the Park. The plaza was dedicated on November 14, 1978.

44. 127 John Street

This building was developer Melvyn Kaufman's answer to the uniform seriousness of downtown. A lobby plaque states, "This building was designed to create an atmosphere of pleasure, humor, and excitement for people." It contains sculptures of a motorcycle and a bicycle, chained to a bike rack, and a high-tech steel tube entryway that has been the background for many print advertisements. The building is surrounded by angular loveseats in bright primary colors and phone booths whose outlines represent callers holding coins. The building includes platforms for children to climb; a long silver fish, in keeping with its seaport vicinity; and the world's largest digital clock, covering the Pearl Street side of the first floor. (The numbers at the top show hours; the rest of the numbers are for minutes and seconds.) Like the wildly lighted air-conditioning room halfway up the building, the lighted clock is best seen at dusk or at night.

45. South Street Seaport

This Historic District is what remains of the days of sail in the first half of the 19th Century, when bowsprits overhung the streets, the smell of fish was in the air, and ships

Fig. 42. South Street, 1880's

from South Street traveled to the Far East, Africa, South America, and around the world. The streets hummed with excitement and business. Shops sold chandler items to be taken on voyages that lasted up to three years. The ships brought back woods, tea, tools, spices, and clothing from around the world, to be sold in New York and shipped across the country.

South Street Ships

* *Peking*, a four-masted bark built in Hamburg, Germany in 1911, for long years traveled the nitrate run to Chile. In the Children's Center a wonderful ten-minute film shows this metal-hulled ship weathering a treacherous storm off Cape Horn 50 years ago. She was strong enough to go "around the

Horn" under sail when other ships had to furl and wait for better weather. She ran the nitrate run until 1931 when chemical fertilizers dropped the price of nitrates. Then the *Peking* became a stationary training ship until she was bought by the South Street Seaport Museum.

Fig. 43. A Clipper

* The full-rigged merchantman *Wavertree* was built in England in 1885, and often carried nitrate for fertilizer. She lost a mast off Cape Horn in 1910, and was kept in Chile as something of a floating warehouse until she was bought in 1967 for South Street.

* The *Ambrose* was the Coast Guard's first Ambrose Channel lightship, from 1908-36 marking the channel into New York harbor. In 1968, four years after being replaced by a Coast Guard lighthouse, she came to South Street as the Museum's first acquisition.

* The *Alexander Hamilton* is the last of the Hudson River Day Line sidewheelers.

* The *Lettie G. Howard*, a Gloucester fishing schooner, is the oldest clipper-bowed fishing schooner left in America. Built in Massachusetts in 1893, she was too small to carry the engines of her day, so she is a pure sailing ship. Designed for speed, she went where the fish were and returned to shore as quickly as possible with the freshest catch.

South Street Buildings

Buildings remain from times past, many in continuous use for almost 200 years. The Joseph Rose House at 273 Water Street was built in 1773. This is the oldest commercial building in

Manhattan, and the third oldest building of any kind on the island. It has had a variety of uses. Rose was a mariner. By 1785 he was a distiller. His son Isaac ran an apothecary here from 1796 to 1807. By 1860 the building had become a saloon, its clients called by an 1868 missionary publication "the most depraved and infamous" in Manhattan. The building has barely survived. In 1904 a fire destroyed the building's third floor and roof; the front and rear walls were raised to the ridge of the old peaked roof. In 1976 a derelict lighting a fire started a blaze that gutted the building.

* Schermerhorn Row includes, 2-18 Fulton St., 91, 92, 93 South Street, and 195 and 197 Front Street. The seventeen buildings that comprise this Georgian-Federal and Greek Revival style composite are the last surviving row of Federal-style warehouses left in New York City, the oldest row of houses remaining in Manhattan. They were built by Peter Schermerhorn, a chandler at 243 Water Street, on water lots, land above water at low tide but submerged at high tide. To reclaim this

Fig. 44. Map of South Street Seaport Area

land from the river, wooden cribs filled with dirt and refuse were laid out on it. The buildings Schermerhorn erected on this landfill were rented out and never used by his family. Two buildings may date from before 1793. Thirteen were created in 1811 and 1812; three were built in the mid-1830s; the last one was erected in 1850. They were built as countinghouses to serve the merchants whose profits came from shipping.

The corner building, a steamboat hotel called McKinley's and later called the Fulton Ferry Hotel, once housed merchants in on buying trips. Although in 1968 the row was marked for demolition, the Landmarks Preservation Commission saved it. In 1974 it was bought by New York State for restoration.

The best known business in Schermerhorn Row is Sweet's Restaurant on the second floor of 4 Fulton Street since 1847, where even slave ship captains used to dine. Founded by Abraham M. Sweet, who called it a refectory, it contained its original pressed-rosewood walls, bare ash and oak floors, and some sea memorabilia until a terrible fire gutted it at the beginning of 1982.

* New Bogardus Building, 19 Fulton Street. Built in 1983, this building commemorates the first Cast Iron building in New York, the Edgar Laing Stores. Designed by James Bogardus, the Laing Stores stood in the vicinty of the Washington Market. Dismantled in 1971 to be reerected later, they were stolen for scrap metal.

Cast Iron was the popular covering for Manhattan commercial buildings from 1848 through the end of the century. The process was to make a mold of a single element of a building--a column, a leaf of the capital--and then pour molten iron into the cast to create however many of that element were wanted. Like other forms of

Fig. 45. Cast Iron Sections

industrialization that transformed life in the 19th Century, the process replaced skilled and artistic labor. Instead of hiring relatively expensive stonecutters, a merchant had just to select elements for the new facade from an iron foundry catalogue. In a matter of days or weeks, the iron parts would be delivered to the site and bolted onto the old brick facade. Although few could afford an authentic stone building, because now each element could be so easily produced many business owners bought cast iron facades for a more expensive look. Not two columns, but ten, twenty, forty fit the age of increasing wealth and growth.

* Museum Visitor's Center at 207 Water Street provides museum information and admissions. The bulding is a good example of classic New York waterfront and commercial architecture of the first half of the 19th century. It was built in the Greek Revival style.

* Bowne & Co., Stationers at 211 Water Street occupies a building dating from 1835-36 whose first tenant was a tin and metals warehouse. The present store is named for a business founded in 1775 by Robert Bowne, an American

of four generations and a Quaker. The business had been at 39 Queen Street (Pearl St.) and sold quite a variety of goods--American writing papers, account books, pens, binding and printing materials, bolted cloths, powder, furs, nails, glass, dry goods, pitch pine boards, and cutlery. After the Revolution, Bowne took on printing jobs. He would have printed the broadside notices announcing ship arrivals and departures and supplied storekeepers with ledgers, financial forms, and stationery supplies, a common combination at the time.

Today, Bowne & Co. is a major financial printer with headquarters in lower Manhattan. The Robert Bowne Foundation funded the re-creation of this 19th-Century Print Shop, which today sells inks, hand-printed cards, and bookmarks--while a display of over a dozen antique printing presses can be viewed on the second floor.

* The Seaport Gallery at 213 Water Street was also a tin and metals warehouse for the many stove makers in the district. Today the gallery displays selections from the museum's

permanent collection of paintings, ship models, and nautical artifacts.

* A.A. Low Building at 171 John Street. This firm of A.A. Low and Brothers was leader of the glamorous China Trade, with a fleet of China clippers built for them, including Houqua, Montauk, Surprise, and Oriental. Their trade of fabrics, porcelains, spices, and teas from China and Japan helped fuel the prosperity of New York in the Nineteenth Century. The firm occupied its building here on Burling Slip from 1850 until after the turn of the century.

* The *trompe l'oeil* mural at Peck Slip was painted by the artist Richard Haas on the blank wall of the Con Edison substation. It evokes some of the past of the area. One of its low buildings is called Swiftsure Express; its Brooklyn Bridge is just to the left of the actual bridge. Unfortunately, some authentic buildings which the picture replicates were demolished for the present building.

* The wholesale Fulton Fish Market has been on the site since 1834,

Fig. 46. Perch

established to "supply the common people with the necessities of life at a reasonable price." Originally one could buy there not only fish, but also cheap finery, books, ice cream, candy, even hardware and dry goods, and oysters from the oyster bars. Today 1500 people work here to sell 250 species of fish. At 4 or 5 in the morning, the sellers can be visited as they dispose of their wares to retail fish markets and restaurants around town.

Conclusion

In the bustling and vibrant southern tip of Manhattan, the part of the island where it all began, many remnants of New York's earliest days remain. Trinity is there with its graves of infants, young women, and early patriots. The site of Washington's inauguration can be seen, along with the old fort that housed both Jenny Lind and 8 million arriving immigrants. The slips and old countinghouses still survive at South Street, part of a great restoration project. All the remnants add a sense of depth and history to the speed, change, and energy of the area today.

Selected Bibliography

Bolton, Reginald Pelham. *Indian Life of Long Ago in the City of New York.* New York: Crown Publishers, 1972.

Butler, the Rev. John V., Rector. *Churchyards of Trinity Parish in the City of New York 1697-1969.* New York: Corporation of Trinity Church, 1948, 1955, 1969.

Edmiston, Susan and Cirino, Linda D. *Literary New York.* Boston: Houghton Mifflin Company, 1976.

Fischler, Stan. *Uptown, Downtown: A Trip Through Time on New York's Subways.* New York: Hawthorn Books, Inc.

Gayle, Margot, and Gillon, Edmund V., Jr. *Cast-Iron Architecture in New York.* New York: Dover, 1974.

Goldberger, Paul. *The City Observed: New York.* New York: Vintage Books/Random House, 1979.

Goldstone, Harmon H., and Darymple, Martha. *History Perserved-A Guide to New York City Landmarks and Historic Districts.* New York: Simon and Schuster, 1974.

Goodwin, Maud Wilder; Royce, Alice Carrington; and Putnam, Ruth. *Historic New York-The Half Moon Papers.* New York: The Knickerbocker Press/G.P. Putnam's Sons, 1897.

Grinstein, Hyman B. *The Rise of the Jewish Community of New York 1654-1860.* Phildelphia: The Jewish Publication Society of America, 1945.

Huxtable, Ada Louise. *Classic New York: Georgian Gentility to Greek Elegance.* Garden City, N.Y.: Anchor Books/Doubleday & Co., Inc., 1964.

King, Moses. *King's Handbook of New York 1893, Vol. I.* Boston: Moses King, 1893; reprint Ed., New York: Benjamin Blom, Inc., 1972.

Lyman, Susan Elizabeth. *The Story of New York.* New York: Crown Publishers, Inc., 1964.

Morehouse, Clifford P. Trinity: *Mother of Churches.* New York: The Seabury Press, 1973.

Post, John J.*Old Streets, Roads, Lanes, Piers and Wharves of New York.* New York: R.D. Cooke, 1882.

Postal, Bernard and Koppman, Leonel. *Jewish Landmarks in New York.* New York: Hill and Wang, 1964.

Rosebrock, Ellen Fletcher. *Counting-house Days in South Sreet: New York's Early Brick Seaport Buildings.* New York: South Street Seaport Museum, 1975.

___ *Farewell to Old England: New York in Revolution.* New York: South Street Seaport Museum, 1976.

___ *Walking Around in South Street.* New York: South Street Seaport Museum, 1975.

Shackleton, Robert. *The Book of New York.* Philadelphia: The Penn Publishing Co., 1917.
Shumway, Floyd M. *Seaport City: New York in 1775.* New York: South Street Seaport Museum, 1975.
Stokes, Isaac Newton Phelps. *The Iconography of Manhattan Island, 1498-1909.* New York, R.H. Dodd, 1915-28.
White, Norval and Willensky, Elliot. *AIA Guide to New York City.* New York: Collier Books, 1967, 1978.
Wolfe, Gerard R. *New York, A Guide to the Metroplis: Walking Tours of Architecture and History.* New York: New York University Press, 1975.
van der Zee, Henri and van der Zee, Barbara. *A Sweet and Alien Land: The Story of Dutch New York.* New York: The Viking Press, 1978.

Illustrations

Charles B. Todd, *A Brief History of the City of New York,* 1899;
American Book Co.; Figs. 1, 3, 10, 11, 13, 20, 22, 23, 31, 37, 39, 43;
New York Public Library, Prints Div.; Fig. 2;
*Historic New York; The Half Moon Series,*eds. Maud Wilder Goodwin, Alice Carrington Royce, Ruth Putnam, and Eva Palmer Brownell, 1901; G.P. Putnam's Sons; Fig. 4; Felix Oldboy, *A Tour around New York,* 1893; Harper & Bros. Figs. 6, 7, 36;
Caroline D. Emerson, *Old New York for Young New Yorkers,* 1932; E.P. Dutton & Co., Inc.; Copyright E.P. Dutton & Co., Inc., 1932, by permission of the publisher; Figs. 14, 33, 40;
Harper's Weekly; Dec. 8, 1883, Fig. 15; Oct. 16, 1869, Fig. 18;
Courtesy of The New York State Historical Association, Cooperstown; Fig. 9;
Courtesy of the Harry T. Peters Collection of The Museum of the City of New York; Fig. 26;
Frank Leslie's Illustrated Newspaper, June 20, 1885; Fig. 28;
Courtesy of The Seamen's Church Institute; Figs. 29, 42;
Courtesy of The New-York Historical Society; Fig. 32;
Courtesy of The Home Insurance Co., Inc.; Fig. 35;
Courtesy of Congregation Shearith-Israel; fig. 38;
Daniel Badger, *Badger's Illustrated Catalogue of Cast-Iron Architecture,* 1981; Dover Publications, Inc.; Fig. 45
Courtesy of the Federal Reserve Bank of N.Y.; Fig. 41;
Courtesy of the South Street Seaport Museum; Fig. 44;

The author is grateful for permission to reprint from the following:
AIA Guide to New York City by Norval White and Elliot Willensky, copyright 1967, 1968 by New York Chapter, American Institute of Architects, copyright 1978 by Norval White and Elliot Willensky; published by Macmillan Publishing Co., Inc. and reprinted with their permission.
The City Observed: New York by Paul Goldberger, copyright 1979; reprinted by permission of Random House, Inc.
Seamen's Church Institute of New York and New Jersey, a Brief History published by The Seamen's Church Institute and reprinted with their permission.

Index